Cotton Candy Coated Chocolate Kisses:
Black Gay Love Poems

Malcolm C. Varner

Cover Art by
Julian J. Gardea

Dedication

To same-gender-loving men of color. The choice to love ourselves belongs to us and no one else. Let us therefore choose wisely without apology.

Acknowledgments

God is owed my profound thanks for giving me life and the wherewithal to complete this work, which is a confirmation of same-gender-loving Black men and our romantic expressions. Secondly, I have to thank my lifelong mentor, John Ravenna, for helping me realize early on that accepting who I was as a gay man was vital to my livelihood rather than an option. It was a journey getting there, but that is one river I've been able to cross. Naturally, some appreciation is also due to the few men that I have loved thus far. In each case, I've learned important lessons on love, communication, vulnerability, honesty, hurt, pride, and passion – all of which are elements careened throughout this collection. Lastly, countless thanks are in order to the endearing same-gender-loving women and men I've met who have personified commitment, parenthood, communication, love, and honor in their everyday lives. You are heroes to us all.

"Love him and let him love you. Do you think anything else under heaven really matters?"
James Baldwin

Contents

A.M.

To arise at each dawn
And find you near is
Like drinking from the
Fountain of youth -
As you are thirst quenching
And life giving.

To embrace you in the
Warmth of our sheets is
Like taking in serenity
Before storms wreak havoc -
As our stillness inspires
Peace before each day.

To send you off daily
With a long kiss is
Like a mother's love
Toward her children -
As she prays to God
For their safe return.

Baise-Moi

Your kiss is like CPR to me.
With lips touching softly,
Your breath awakens my senses
And I become a living being. Alive,
As your breath flows down
My checks and the stubble
On your face caresses my chin –
Thru this closeness we exchange life.
Your hands have a magician's
Touch, disappearing into my shirt
And resurfacing to my head. They keep
Me guessing with eyes closed,
Waiting for the thrill of your next trick.
As we draw closer, blissfully our lips
Yield to the dance of our tongues,
Watering every crevice of our mouths
With sweet wonderment.
The taste of your lips is like
Chocolate kisses wrapped in
Cotton candy – an irresistible treat.
The more you press in and
Softly suckle my lower lip,
I return the pleasing favor.
And in your grasp my body temperature
Elevates to fire, one that you alone
Can extinguish.
But for now, these flames
Do not need to be put out.
For I am intoxicated by
The smoke of our passion
That you started by placing
Your mouth on mine and
Kissing me like eternity was ours.

Beauty

We met, and instantly
Connection happened,
Naturally. Beyond his
Rich dark skin and bald
Head I secretly refer
To as my private and
Chocolate delight is a heart
And soul immersed in
Rare honesty. Challenged
By the sensitivity of his
Very being, love willingly
And openly tugged at me.
It was a gentle, yet sure pull,
Incomparable to any other
Romantic rapport that used
To be. For unlike the others
This man looked into me, and
Seeing everything that could
Be, supported and pushed me
To release the boiling lava of
Book-bound and simmering
Words onto blank surfaces with my
Pen. With blue ink oozing onto
Paper creating another poem
That he has inspired, like

The scrolls of scripture by men
Called by God to write for man's sake,
Yet God's divine purpose.
His love keeps my heart anchored
As I learn to let go of
Counterfeit intentions and
Promises of the past.
For his being is true,
And he is true to his being.
And as with poetry, the more
I get to know him, his human
Perfection is crystalized
In my heart and eyes.

Black & Gay

Being black is bad enough they say,

Just don't be black *and* gay.

The world is tough alone with racial prejudice,

But for a queer black man, even more inclement.

Unnaturally sinful they describe this way,

But I'd rather be honest than to ever dare betray.

Sometimes it seems folks would prefer me to be DL,

Leaving my woman and kids with a sad story to tell

Of how I lied to be with her and

Secretly longed that she was sir.

Whether 'tis nature or nature,

I do not care.

Knowing this fact would nothing change.

For I'd still be me, gay and black – all the same.

It was hard but I've managed to reconcile.

Put me in exile, but I won't dare live in denial.

Circumstances

It all seemed so simple at first.
We met online to chill
And have a good time.
Without hidden agendas
Or preconceived notions,
It was one of those things
Where it was what it was.
But Fate can be twisted
By turning such encounters
Into bittersweet moments
Where two potentially kindred
Souls are forced apart.
And that's what she did.
Our "no strings attached"
Plan was upheaved by Fate's
Arms while unforeseen feelings
Took ahold of us both.
Beyond his carnal beauty
I began the process of knowing
His inner-man – dreams and
Yearnings, goals and strengths,
Shortcomings and corks –
In the days to come we had to together.
This exchange was mutual,
As I even shared parts of myself.

But regrettably, I also knew

That Fate was cruelly

Conspiring against us.

For in a matter of days

Many miles would

Separate us, and our lives

Would go on as they had.

So all we can do now is

Cherish this brevity,

While surrendering ourselves

To the hope and chance that

Fate knows what's best

Since now it's not so simple anymore.

Confirmation

One. Two. Three...
I counted the
Times that you
Tapped your
Air Force One
Across the
Squeaky-clean
White clinic
Floor. As your
Left palm
Secreted sweat
Into mine and
Tiny water droplets
Formed on your
Forehead, it
Dawned upon me
That we had made
The right decision.
Instead of giving
Ourselves over
To our manhood
Desires, we gave
Ourselves the
Past four months
To ensure that

Our coming

Together was

Not rushed.

I'm glad we did.

Slowly the

Second hand

Of the clock

In the small

Testing room

Ticked. There

Was only the

Sound of our

Thoughts in

The enclosed

Space. As I

Watched your

Shoe tap up

And down, I

Resolved that

Your result

Would not

Change my

Feelings or

Interest in you,

Hoping you felt the same.

(I already knew mine.)

Thus our step today
Is not a deal
Breaker, but
More like a
Step toward
Mutual
Understanding
As we move
Forward together.
As the oak door
Door spun and
The nurse entered,
Our hands
Clasped tighter.
With two files
In hand, she read
One at a time,
"HIV-negative."
Then you kissed me,
Confirming upon
Me again that we
Had made the right
Decision. But,
We can't just stop here.
As we move forward,
Our safety is a must.

And when we
Reach that goal,
Your right foot
Can relax just a
Little bit more
Next time,
Knowing there is
No need to worry.

Crush

Through beats blasting,
Bodies bumping and grinding,
Lights jolting the club's dimness,
Drinks – sipped and splattered
On sticky, sneaker stained tiles –
Thirsty eyes staring askew,
Caddy cliques standing in circles,
Your swag and handsome face stood apart.
From across the dance floor
You stood preying on the wall,
So dominant with the fiercest eyes.
And as I rocked to the house beats,
The midnight skin on your face drew me in
Towards you like gravity pulling the moon.
I wanted to inundate you with kisses
And allow you to explore my creators.
So slowly I moved towards you,
Never missing a beat,
To only be more captivated
By the fullness of your beard,
Thick lips, and snow white smile.
Yet unmoved, you remained tall and still in
Your black fitted cap and clothes.
Boy, my imagination ran amuck!
When your eyes met mine,

Separated now only by a few paces,

I smiled and baited my body

To hook you along for a ride.

You watched me on the low.

My hips jolted left, right, left.

My pelvis popped and shook teasingly, as

My posterior boasted the curves in my pants.

Perplexed by your gazing eyes

And your frozen posture,

I asked you to dance,

Thinking shyness was your vice.

So when you replied, "No, I'm good,"

And then walked away,

A piece of my ego was crushed.

Embracing My Divinity

Beyond my mortal flesh
Lies a splendid soul, a spirit,
A like reflection of the Creator.
Greater than the ashes
That ultimately become of all men
Days after their last hour,
My eternal being is my true essence.

Beyond my mortal flesh,
Faults and all, lies myself in its purest form.
It's my direct connection to the Creator,
The originator of all life and all things.
And from this source I daily draw strength
That pushes me forward each passing day,
Enabling my eyes to see that there is always a way.

Beyond my mortal flesh
Lies a well of power, my true life.
It reminds me that I am greater than strife,
It replenishes my cup with living water, with life.
It gives me courage to fight for my dreams to take flight.
In spite of what happens to my physical man,
My spirit lets me know at all times that I can.

Family Reunion

It was the same routine every year:
The sweltering park in Charlotte,
Your aunt's self-proclaimed famous
Potato salad, a live replaying of
Bebe's Kids, and the ambiguous
Introduction of me as "your boi."
Year five precluded the need to
Practice. You and I we're play-
Off pros by now. If it were
Anyone else, though, I would
Have quit this game of truth
Dodging and weaving eons back.
Your devoted love to me each
Day, our home, and our friends,
Was genuine and thus I knew
Where your heart lied -
Your family, sadly, did not.
And yet, listening to the words
"My boi," was like hearing an
Explosion right in front of me, both
Deafening and blinding.
This year would be no different.
The best I could do was prepare
Myself for this strategic betrayal.

We arrived and as usual,
It was typical North Carolina
Weather in August – hellish.
Green and yellow balloons
Surrounded the welcoming
Sign to the 24th Douglas
Family Reunion, a significant
Achievement in itself.
As you drove slowly to the
Picnic area, Bebe's lot
Played in the grass and those
Who recognized your car waved.

As you parked, my throat
Quenched for a glass of
Fresh lemonade that I saw on
The picnic table moments ago.
There in your car –
Like the times before – you squeezed
My left hand and said, "This is it."
"Let's go," I replied and we made
Our way over the shaded area
Where familiar faces congregated.
The smell of hamburgers, ribs,
And burnt hot dogs teased my stomach
As we approached the crowd.
"Being thirsty and hungry is no
Way to prepare for war,"
I thought to myself.

A series of hellos and hugs
Were shared once we arrived.
And then you spoke....
"You all remember my
Boyfriend, right"? Did I
Hear you correctly?
Judging by their blushing
And mouth dropping faces,
With as much Christian
Friendliness as possible, I
Surmised so. "Of course
We remember him," said
Your cousin Tooty,
Breaking up the temporary
Silence that overcame us all.
"Welcome to the family chile," she
Continued as she hugged me
Again. This moment set off
An explosion of different sorts.
Though partially numb from
Surprise, my heart was
Racing with a rare pride,

Not for me but for you.
Watching you smile as
Your authentic self was
A true delight; it's one
Of those moments we'll
Treasure for years ahead.
Finally, it was time for some
Lemonade. And as I got a
Little more settled, I thought
To myself while looking at the
Food, "Maybe your aunt's potato
Salad will actually be okay this year."

Forbidden Fruit

Our love is a yin-yang taboo;
A bold and intricate face tattoo;
A reminder of Jim Crow history -
Now a modern mystery —
It challenges racial oppression
With the twist of our sexual expression.

Our love is an Othello production,
An object of conspired destruction.
Our clasped hands inspire rolled eyes
And hurtful quick goodbyes
From those who loved us the most,
Who now say everything, but of us boast.

Our love is a throw of dice,
A gamble for which we sacrifice
Our livelihood and all that we know;
Our love is too risky to be for show.
It's a test, tried and true,
Blind to race, color, or hue.

Fortress

After a day's travail
I come home to you,
And I exhale, thankful
For our abode, buffering
Us from a bi-polar
And polarized world.
Our home is an oasis
Where daily we retreat,
Where our lives are lived
In congruence, and
Where dissonance and
Division have no belonging.
I find you upon arrival waiting
Patiently to welcome me
With a familiar kiss
Like from yesterday
And the day before.
Immediately we chat and
Your laughter gives
My mind a deep tissue massage,
Easing tension built up from outside.
I'm comforted knowing the walls
Of our house block out jeers of "fag"
And other epithets that, if accepted
On the inside, would implode our home.

You, my dear, equip me with the strength
To rise everyday just as I am,
Unconcerned with those who willingly
Choose not to understand us.
At each day's dawning, your love cradles me
In the palms of your hands
And presents me like a gift for a king,
So precious a treasure, a jewel
To be seen and protected.

Lifetime

If these old walls could talk
Silence would be forever
Threatened because of
The life we've shared.
If these old walls could talk
They'd speak of traditions
Of white Christmas trees
And tomato red stockings
Hung perfectly down
Maplewood staircases.
If these old walls could talk
They'd reminisce of anniversaries
Spent privately with
Bottles of Italian-imported
Merlot and white chocolate
Mints shared on
Our favorite couch and blanket.
If these old walls could talk
They'd speak of fried
Chicken, collard greens,
Black-eyed peas, and
Golden-brown crusted
Cornbread cooked on
Sundays and shared
Amongst merry friends.

If these old walls could talk
They'd dearly recall fallen
Tears on tissues, held
By mourners dawned
In black suits, dresses,
Suede stilettos and loafers.
If these old walls could talk
They'd extoll the three
Years of rearing your
Nephew when his mother
Was in prison, recovering from
Alcohol and her own misdeeds.
If these old walls could talk
They'd lose track of counting
The litany of laughs and
Smiles that brought our
Once new home to life.
If these old walls could talk
We'd sit and listen to their
Endless stories, never
Regretting a single moment.

Love is

Love is Sundays spent at church
Service sitting next to each other –
Praying, praising, and worshiping.
Love is holding your hand at the
Movies, while you rest your head
On my shoulder as you fall asleep.
Love is bringing you breakfast
In bed on Saturdays and watching
You eat until you're satisfied and full.
Love is birthdays and anniversaries
Remembered with colorful squiggly
Marks on the calendar of our refrigerator.
Love is forgiveness after disagreements
And misdeeds that were hard to get over.
Love is countless Facebook posts
Of us smiling and being who we are –
It's our public declaration that says
I'm in a relation with you.
Love is tying your tie and saying
"Have a great day, baby" as you
Leave for work five days a week.
Love is fried fish on Fridays at our
Favorite soul food restaurant and
Sharing a slice of cheesecake afterwards.
Love is hosting monthly dinner parties for
Our friends that never end before midnight.
Love is fixing up tomato soup and tall
Glasses of OJ as you lie sick in bed.
It's holding you close to me when
We're watching scary movies on the sofa.
Love is me being there for you after
The death of your mom, your best friend.
Love is knowing what you're thinking
Before you say a word;
It's laughing hysterically with you
When you goof up somehow.
Love is singing to you in the shower

And massaging your body after workouts.
Love is sacrificing for our dream home
And appreciating what we have today.
Love is an outpouring of our complementary
Lives. It's a choice that we've freely made
And the reason our lives are blessed.

More

I want to get to know you more.
Like a European gamer on an African safari,
 I want to explore
Your vast, broad, grassy, and hot lands
With the curious digits of my two hands.
I want to ride across your brave and naked fields,
While feeling the fortitude of your earth inside me as I yield
To your terrain.
I want you to beckon unto me underneath the starry night
To nibble your tongue and just be still,
So our love is not uncovered by foreigners
Or curious creators whose big nocturnal eyes could spot us
From afar.
As magnificent as your bronze body is,
You'd quickly hide like a hermit crab in its shell if you were
Found,
Leaving me alone and shivering in our combined sweat from
Their cold stares.
So with my mouth gripping your callous thumb,
I'd secretly hope that nothing would come between us.
I'd acquiesce, lying still, with our mouths joined together
Underneath the black jeweled landscape speckled with blues
And purples.
On that night we'd give nature herself something to envy –
An act by and for which we were created.
That is all that I want.

More Than

I am more than a label,
More than any diagnosis,
I am everything that makes me able
To fight despite dismal prognosis.
I am more than HIV,
The harsh reality of PTSD,
The nodding disorder of narcolepsy,
The crippling of cerebral palsy,
The progression of muscular atrophy,
Or even the fate of living blindly.
Whatever the label may therefore be
It'll do you no good to limit me.
For the reality, you see,
Is that I am full of deeper complexity:
For truthfully, I am a sea of possibility
Where labels sink below endlessly
To a dark empty floor where they belong.
I am more than a label
More than any diagnosis,
I am everything that makes me able
To fight despite dismal prognosis.
I am a fighter! I am both human
And spirit, and any label that
Fails to capture this fact
Isn't worthy of my time.

My Answer to "So, What's Your Type?"

More than anything,
A man who can be
True to me.
A man who won't
Serenade me with lies
Or sell me fake promises;
He'll simply tell the truth.
A grown man who
Doesn't pretend
That he will if he can't.
He'll have the courage to
Be open and upfront instead
Of saying sorry or
Making excuses later.
A man who will let me
Love him for who he is.
He's bold enough to remove
His shades and
Wear something
Comfortable; he doesn't
Dress to impress for
He recognizes that
Honesty needs
No disguise.
A man okay

With being nude
In plain daylight
Where there's no
Room for doubt,
And then who will fully let
Me admire and
Embrace his being -
Perfections, scars,
And all.
If he can do all these things
And still be okay,
Then he must be true
To himself.
Such is a man
That I'll gladly
Call my own.

My Dearest Me

I love you unconditionally.
Let these words penetrate
Every cell and atom of your
Mortal man and throughout
The very essence of your mind
And soul. Yes, I love you.
Yesterday is behind you,
So let it lie there. You've
Proven that you are an overcomer.
Today is your biggest asset –
Use it wisely.
Everyday your mantra should be
"Carpe diem," as well as
Dylan Thomas' words
Resisting the night's call.
At this moment of time just
Give yourself a chance to
Live the fullest life you can:
To embrace stability over
Chaos; to embrace peace over
Confusion; to embrace good company
Over wolves; to uphold what's
Good and beneficial over
Reckless choices; to embrace
Patience over haste; to embrace

Hard work over shortcuts; and to

Promote love over bitterness

And hate alike. These are all choices.

Always keep your eyes high,

Ensuring that your thoughts and

Actions follow suit.

Love others.

Remember and

Honor this fundamental

Human need. I love you,

I love you, and once more,

I love you - and that shall never fail.

Nine Months

Destined to change

In nine precious months,

Our lives will never be the same.

For our abode of two will

Become a home for three

And you and I will extend

To a broader we,

A family that many say

Should never be.

Our hearts, however,

Know differently

And that we could

Never take raising a

Child lightly. No, this

Choice stemmed from

Our matched souls'

Desires to be fathers

Who are present,

Committed, protectors,

And guides in helping

Our kids aspire to

Their best selves. Now

That chance is upon us,

And I'm more certain now

Than ever that were doing

The right thing. Regardless
Of the role-models we
Had, we've proven our
Selves to be different
Already in our lives
And love to one another.
Surely, the honor and
Responsibility before us
Are great, but it is a privilege
To know that this lifelong
Journey of fatherhood
Will be shared with you.

Not for Sale

My name isn't Escort,
Gigolo, Prostitute,
Or your Private Ho.
My name is Not for Sale.

My name isn't Skank,
Whore, Worthless,
Or Desperate Bitch.
My name is Not for Sale.

My name isn't Trade,
Boy for Rent, Seeking Generous,
Or Will Fuck for Money, Food, or Clothes.
My name is Not for Sale.

My name isn't Slut,
Tramp, Scandalous,
Or Hire-for-Tonight.
My name is Not for Sale.

My name isn't Hustler,
Bimbo, Seeking Sugar Daddy,
Or Paid-Piece-of-Tail.
My name is Not for Sale.

My name isn't Dick for Hire,
Trash, Giver of Happy Endings,
Or Streetwalker.
My name is Not for Sale.

My name isn't Hooker,
Harlot, Hussy,
Or Jezebel.
My name is Not for Sale.

My name isn't Pay-then-Leave,
Floozy, Wench,

Or Motel Junkie.
My name is Not for Sale.

My name isn't Strumpet,
Call Boy, Street Worker,
Or Employee of "the oldest profession."
My name is Not for Sale.

My name isn't Trick,
Night Walker, Scum,
Or your Sexual Slave.
My name is Not for Sale.

And don't you forget it!

Not Forgotten

To departed

Uncles,

Sons,

Brothers,

Friends,

Fathers, and

Lovers,

Lives lost to

AIDS,

Rest in peace.

The gift of

Your life

Touched

Those around

You,

Whether many

Or just a few.

Your soul was

A gentle candle

Whose light

Never faltered,

Even while

Each flicker

Faded to smoke.

You graced

Us with humor,

Kindness, fun,

Thoughtfulness,

And love,

Reminding us

That life is precious.

You lived life

On fire

With passion,

Contagious to

Whoever knew you.

Your lived moments

Are now cherished

Memories like

Sweet cherries,

Of which I am

Choosing the best.

Love is greater

Than mistakes or

Regrets, and

As such,

You are someone

I'll love always and could

Never forget.

Online Read

SMH!
Really?
IJS!
You want what from me?
LMAO @ U cuz
You haven't given me
Anything.
Double standards
Aren't my thing -
And that boo
Is the T!

Oh really?
If I go ahead,
You're going to as well?
Now U are giving me
Too much.
Tell me why would I
Want a coward and a
Man who's afraid to lead.
Real talk.
And that boo
Is the T!

See now you mad,
Talking 'bout WTF!
Well that's on U.
You lost in ur
Own game; no shade.
U just stepped
The wrong way.
When U stop playing yo self,
U'll attract some1 else.
And that boo
Is the T!

Priceless

He was blinged out.

His rings sparkled

And flashed like

Disco balls at the club.

His ear-jutted diamonds

Could blind you from

The right angle like

Mirrors reflecting rays

Of light. He had mad

Swag; this I cannot deny.

He rocked True Religion

Denim, limited J's,

Tom Ford belts to

Accessorize his Gucci

Suits, and Louis

Vuitton glasses to

Shade him from the sun.

He drove an S-Class and

Housed a S8 Audi

For weekend excursions

To Miami in his garage.

He lived in a two-story

Condo in Midtown Atlanta,

And had property on

Both coasts. He

Looked as good as
His money and
Smelled even better –
He was rarer than
One in a million.

The problem?
He was all talk.
His words were
Fancy and elegant,
But lacked true
Substance when
It came to his
Deeds. He
Communicated –
To me and all
Around him –
With money and
Expensive gifts, not
Realizing that
Lavish can be
Limited. His
Ears were far
From me, and
Thus was his heart.
He could never

Admit that was

The case, but

His preoccupation

With trivialities

Over my heart

Was all the proof

I needed. He

Listened and spoke

To benefit him;

He was a favor

To those around him.

This was who he was.

I left him with all

Of his possessions.

He taught me that

True value is not

Measured by money alone.

My heart and love

Could never be sold;

They are treasures

To be given at my

Will to a man deserving

Of such. I will know

Him by the integrity

Of his actions

And the words he says.

His ears will also

Speak to my heart;

They will inform me

How he values those

Around him. And

Whether he be

A millionaire or making

Minimum wage,

His heart must be

Honest and sincere.

Promenade

While we are vibing

And feeling the chemistry

That's sparked a flame

We had no idea would ignite,

Let's not get scorched by

Hastiness or infatuation.

Instead, let's take the scenic

Route of love's journey

Where we can walk,

Relaxed, at a tranquil pace.

Let's traverse this road of

Unknown paths and

Natural beauty

With open eyes without GPS

Guiding our every trod, turn, or twist.

No, let's lock in cruise control.

Let's tell tales of favorite friends and

Whisper secrets untold,

While holding hands as we

Explore the countryside before us.

Let's gaze into each other's eyes

With intrigue of the person

We are both discovering.

And when we do not see eyes-to-eye,

Let's listen to seek understanding.

Let's remind ourselves that love
Is an impossible end without risk.
If we can see tenuous moments
As opportunities for fruitful growth –
Like deciduous trees budding
In the spring after a long winter –
Together we can grow, too.
As we walk through this trail
Detached from the world and time alike,
Let's share our ambitions
With the stars themselves
And hold each other for comfort
In the night's still coolness.
And while our destination is largely unknown,
Let's patiently honor this journey with honesty.

Rendezvous

We sat down smiling
On two seats at an Italian bistro,
Sitting face-to-face just close enough
To whisper if we needed such intimacy.
Our table was checkered white and red
With shining utensils peeking out of napkins.
A single votive candle in a petit glass jar
Swayed calmly between you and me,
Following the temperament of laughter and
Elated sounds as we conversed.
I admired the way your hands cupped
Your rounded glass of red wine,
And how you gently sipped with
Lips that I hoped to kiss at the night's
End, marking our adieu.
We talked freely and discovered
Commonalities that are rare to find.
Occasionally our eyes seemed to stop time,
Giving us both the chance to read each other's mind.
You moved and talked so freely,
While I listened intently to what you shared –
You even returned the courtesy.
With the lapse of time and exit of other patrons,
I resisted the thought of ending this experience.
So for tonight I'll settle for your kiss, and

Wishing you sweet dreams in lieu of me holding you.
As for next time, I promise to hold your hand.

Resilient

Try as you might

By laughing at me,

Mocking me,

Ignoring my

Face and yet

Stealing my ideas

With your back

Turned towards

Me, but as for

What's mine,

I won't be denied.

My prize awaits me

Tomorrow.

Try as you might

By tripping me

And then spewing

Lukewarm spit

On me while I'm

Down, kicking me

Or assaulting me

With sticks

And stones to

Break my bones,

But as for

What's mine,

I won't be denied.

My prize awaits me

Tomorrow.

Try as you might

By kicking me out,

Withholding your

Love from me,

Boasting your few

Possessions to make

Me envy you, or

Whispering lies

About me to hide

Your inconvenient

Truth, but as for

What's mine,

I won't be denied.

My prize awaits me

Tomorrow.

Saying "I Do"

We did it, you and I.
Fate has rewarded us well,
Destiny has showed us her fortune,
And heaven has made us complete.
After battling thru years of injustice
And painfully settling for second-class,
We have spoken our "I do's" and
Formalized the commitment of our hearts.
To each other we vowed oneness –
Our marriage was a public declaration.
Eye to eye we stood in anticipation
Of the future we had to cherish
Upon entering our scared union.
Proudly I kissed your dear lips
And gently held your smooth face.
And it was at that magical point
That all of life's pieces fell into place.
We are what fairytales dream about
In their lands of happy endings.
We did it, you and I.

Sick and Tired

We must not accept HIV and AIDS
As inevitable realities due to who we are.
These threats are much less powerful
Than they've become - never forget.
This battle is ours to be won.

We must not accept the darkness
Of depression, anxiety, or despair.
These issues are not ends to themselves
Nor are they all encompassing for anyone.
This battle is ours to be won.

We must not accept drugs, including
Alcohol, as healing aids for those real
Matters stirring within our minds and hearts.
They are false allies upon whom we cannot rely.
This battle is ours to be won.

We must not accept that we are solely
Sexual creatures of well endowment,
Bent towards endless conquests. Such notions
Are historical traps we must despise.
This battle is ours to be won.

We must not accept that poverty

And homelessness are our rightful
Ends in life nor that our destiny is
To endlessly live in plight.
This battle is ours to be won.

We must not accept lives of
Solitude or lies that inform us
That we are incapable of
Long-term and committed love.
This battle is ours to be won.

We must not accept suicide
As a natural or intended end
To our lives gifted with unique
Purpose to be shared.
This battle is ours to be won.

Brothas, let us accept and
Love ourselves for who we are,
Individually and collectively. Let
Us speak, write, and work for change
Until these battles are all overcome.

Silver Lining

Your love is my salvation
From this sickness that lies
Within. In love, you patiently
Sat with me through painful
Crises and moments where
My grasp on life seemed to
Slip beyond my keeping.
Faithfully, you stood by me
And held my hand through
Long troublesome nights
And prayed for my recovery.
In each episodic storm that
Ravaged my inner-man,
You've proven to me just
How much of a man that you
Are – never running from me
Or complaining about this
Unpleasant burden to my soul.
In every case, you've stayed
Relentlessly by my side.
As devastating as it is to
The world we built together,
Somehow we've managed
To both become better.
You are the light in my

Darkest days, allowing me
To see my fears as simple
Shadows and nothing more,
So that I can keep trudging
Onward towards those
Periods of stability and peace
That inevitably come to pass.
And it's during these times
When I am most able to
Express my appreciation for
All that you are to me –
My raison d'être.

Stand

Stand still.
Speak only silence
As I admire you fully.
Your person dwarfs
Greek gods and
Etches a new
Meaning into to
La Negritude
And shouted
Declarations like
"I am Black
And I'm proud."
Yes, you are
A renaissance
Negro, unashamed
To embrace all
Of who you are
In a society
Predicated on
Convenient boxes,
Despite how they
Are universally
Defied.
They are lies.
I smile
Admirably,
As you stand
Black man.
You are truth.
Your actions
And movements
Speak freedom,
Only validated
By your words -
Not vice versa.
You humbly
Teach us lessons

For tomorrow,
Not just today.
Led by your vision,
You forge new
Paths for us all.
Par consequence,
You deserve a
Standing ovation.

Subway

Stairs descending.

Tickets printing.

Gates cycling.

People passing.

Intercoms speaking.

Trains screeching.

Doors sliding.

Passengers boarding.

Lights changing.

Wheels squeaking.

Winds echoing.

Looks exchanging.

People reading.

Earphones blasting.

Smiles exchanging.

Purses shifting.

Riders rocking.

Pleasure exchanging.

Trees passing.

Clouds flying.

Cars darting.

Elbows exchanging.

Cellphone buzzing.

Talkers chatting.

Heads nodding.

Words exchanging.

Driver announcing.

Bodies preparing.

Train screeching.

Numbers exchanging.

Doors sliding.

Passengers existing.

Lights changing.

Wheels squeaking.

Winds echoing.

Looks exchanging.

Waiting

Heart palpitating
Repetitiously -
A little more than
Normal.
Daydreams spur
Me to hope,
But so far,
Only answered by
Anxiety.

Still softly I whisper,
"I am waiting for you."

Ready now
More than ever,
This feeling is
Truth.
The clubs, bars,
And "dating"
Internet sites,
Have been rendered
Lackluster.

So softly I whisper,
"I am waiting for you."

Every day now
Yields a new
Chance for our
Connection.
At that time, we
Won't seem like
Distant strangers
But rather kindred
Spirits.

Until then, softly I whisper,
"I am waiting for you."

Yesterday

The warm sweet taste of his breath
Is as fresh to me as yesterday,
When in reality it has been
Years since our lips pressed
Upon each other's. With eyes closed
He saw into me with his soul
Through our meeting mouths that were
Wide open, with our two tongues colliding
Gently like waves of water.
Yet, it was more than the act of kissing
That drew me into him. It was the
Brushing of my trimmed beard against
His goatee that grew our intimacy,
Pressed upon each other in his queen-size bed
As his football stature put me in place
And I rubbed the baldness of his head
While sweat slowly ran onto his face.
Still sharing breaths between us,
He would hold me close upon his
Bulging brown chest with bristly,
Black and sporadic grey, hair.
Firm in every gesture he made,
His kiss was a pleasing serenade
That put me to sleep after our lips had enough.
And what now seems like only hours ago

Has been multiplied by hours, days,

Months and years,

Remains only a memory.

About the Author

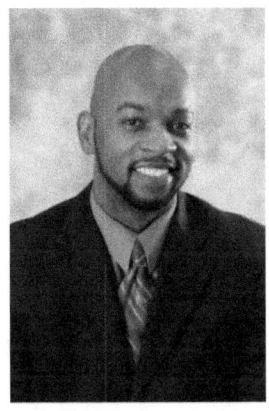

Malcolm O. Varner, licensed social worker, author and mental health advocate, resides in Dallas, TX. He is the author of *Looking Beyond the Storm: Selections of Poetry*, *Creating Positive Ripples: 100 Messages of Encouragement*, and *Looking Beyond the Storm: Now the Rainbow is Out*. Additionally, Malcolm's work has appeared in publications such as *The Columbus African American News Journal* and *Truth* magazine. He holds a BA in religion from Oberlin College and his MSSA from Case Western Reserve University, where he studied community and social development.

www.ingramcontent.com/pod-product-compliance
Lightning Source LLC
Chambersburg PA
CBHW071803170526
45167CB00003B/1147